HOW TO SELL ON eBay 2024

From Zero to eBay Hero – Transforming Your Spare Time into Profit with a Home-Based Reselling Business (A Practical Blueprint for Success)

WAYNE WHITE

Copyright © 2024 Wayne White

Table Of Contents

INTRODUCTION

Welcome and Brief Overview

Embark on a transformative journey into the heart of eBay reselling with "eBay Mastery 2024: From Zero to eBay Hero." As we stand at the precipice of a new era in eCommerce, this book extends a warm welcome to aspiring eBay entrepreneurs seeking not just success but mastery in the intricate art of online reselling.

In this introductory segment, we set the stage for the exploration that follows, offering a tantalizing glimpse into the exciting world of eBay reselling. From the dawn of innovative strategies to the dusk of successful case studies, this book is your compass, navigating the dynamic landscape of eBay in 2024.

The Current Landscape of eBay in 2024

Dive deep into the pulse of eBay as it beats in the year 2024. This section is more than a snapshot; it's an immersive exploration of the nuances shaping the current eBay ecosystem. Uncover the trends, challenges, and unprecedented opportunities that define eBay's terrain, providing you with a comprehensive understanding of the ever-evolving marketplace.

As eBay continues to evolve, so does the potential for entrepreneurs to carve their path to success. Whether you're a newcomer navigating the initial stages or a seasoned seller adapting to the latest trends, this segment provides a holistic view of the eBay landscape, setting the tone for the mastery that awaits.

Why This Book is Essential for Aspiring eBay Entrepreneurs

In the vast sea of reselling guides, why should aspiring eBay entrepreneurs choose this book? This segment answers that question, outlining the unique value proposition that "eBay Mastery 2024" brings to the table.

It's not just a guide; it's a strategic companion designed to meet the diverse needs of eBay enthusiasts.

From the foundational aspects that cater to newcomers to the advanced strategies that propel seasoned sellers forward, this book encapsulates the essence of eBay entrepreneurship in 2024. Aspiring eBay entrepreneurs are invited not only to learn but to master the art of reselling, using this book as a roadmap to navigate the challenges and seize the opportunities that eBay presents in the current era.

As we embark on this journey together, anticipate not only insights and strategies but a comprehensive blueprint that transforms novices into eBay heroes. Welcome to "eBay Mastery 2024," where the future of your reselling success begins.

Beyond the Horizon

Navigating the Intricacies of eBay Mastery:

Within the pages of "eBay Mastery 2024," readers are not just consumers of information but active participants in a comprehensive exploration of eBay's ever-shifting landscape. As we delve into the intricacies of eBay mastery, each chapter becomes a stepping stone, guiding you through the uncharted territories of successful reselling in the year 2024.

Discover the Art of Transformation:

This book is more than a manual; it's a transformative experience. Engage with the content not merely as a passive reader but as an entrepreneur sculpting their path to success. Uncover the art of transformation – turning aspirations into actionable strategies, spare time into profitable endeavors, and uncertainties into triumphs.

A Blueprint Tailored to Your Journey:

In a market inundated with generic advice, "eBay Mastery 2024" distinguishes itself by offering a blueprint that adapts to your unique journey. Whether you're a newcomer looking to establish your eBay presence or a seasoned seller aiming for exponential growth, each chapter is curated to cater to your specific needs, aspirations, and challenges.

Unlock the Power of Knowledge:

Knowledge is the currency of success in the digital age. "eBay Mastery 2024" not only imparts knowledge but empowers you to harness its potential. From the basics of setting up your eBay seller account to the intricacies of leveraging data analytics, this book opens the door to a wealth of information essential for eBay entrepreneurs striving for excellence.

Join a Community of eBay Heroes:

Embarking on this journey is not a solitary endeavor. As you immerse yourself in the content, you're invited to join a community of like-minded individuals – a network of eBay heroes-in-the-making. Share insights, seek advice, and celebrate victories together, fostering a collaborative spirit that enhances the learning experience.

Embrace the eBay Revolution:

In the pages that follow, be prepared to not just read about eBay's evolution but to actively participate in the eBay revolution. This is more than a book; it's a call to action. Whether you're aiming for financial independence, entrepreneurial success, or simply seeking to stay ahead in the ever-shifting eCommerce landscape, "eBay Mastery 2024" is your guide, your mentor, and your companion on the road to eBay heroism. Welcome to a journey where transformation meets triumph, and mastery becomes a reality.

CHAPTER 1

The eBay Advantage in 2024

In the ever-expansive universe of eCommerce, eBay emerges not merely as a platform but as a powerful player shaping the future of online retail. This chapter delves into the multifaceted advantages that eBay offers in 2024, presenting a holistic understanding of its pivotal role in the modern eCommerce ecosystem.

1.1 Understanding the Power of eBay in the Modern eCommerce Ecosystem:

At the core of eBay's influence lies its unparalleled reach and diversity. In 2024, eBay continues to serve as a nexus connecting buyers and sellers across the globe. Its user-friendly interface, expansive product categories, and a vast customer base make it a dynamic marketplace that transcends geographical boundaries. Aspiring eBay entrepreneurs are not merely joining a platform; they are tapping into a global eCommerce phenomenon.

eBay's adaptability is another facet that sets it apart. With continuous updates and improvements, eBay remains at the forefront of technological advancements, offering sellers innovative tools and features to enhance their reselling experience. This section navigates the intricate features of eBay that contribute to its prominence, positioning it as a cornerstone for success in the ever-evolving eCommerce landscape.

1.2 Overview of Opportunities and Challenges in 2024

Success in the world of eBay reselling requires a nuanced understanding of both the opportunities that abound and the challenges that must be navigated. In 2024, the opportunities are as diverse as the products listed on the platform. From the burgeoning trend of niche markets to the integration of cutting-edge technologies, eBay offers resellers an expansive canvas to paint their success stories.

However, where there is opportunity, challenges also emerge. This section provides a detailed overview of the challenges eBay entrepreneurs may encounter in 2024, ranging from increased competition to the ever-changing algorithms dictating search rankings. By acknowledging and understanding these challenges, aspiring sellers are better equipped to formulate strategic approaches and fortify their businesses against potential hurdles.

1.3 Case Studies: Success Stories in the Current eBay Marketplace

Beyond theories and concepts, this chapter breathes life into the possibilities that eBay holds by presenting real-world case studies. These success stories are more than illustrations; they are narratives of resilience, innovation, and strategic prowess in the current eBay marketplace. By delving into the experiences of these eBay entrepreneurs, readers gain practical insights into the diverse paths that lead to success.

From sellers who have mastered the art of cross-border trade to those who have harnessed the power of social commerce, these case studies provide a blueprint for navigating the challenges and seizing the opportunities that eBay presents in 2024. Each success story serves as both inspiration and a practical guide, showcasing the potential for resellers to carve their niche and thrive within the eBay ecosystem.

In unraveling the eBay advantage in 2024, this chapter not only imparts knowledge but fuels the entrepreneurial spirit, inviting readers to see eBay not just as a platform but as a gateway to unlimited possibilities.

CHAPTER 2

Getting Started: A Blueprint for Beginners

Embarking on your eBay journey requires more than just enthusiasm; it demands a strategic and informed approach. In "Getting Started: A Blueprint for Beginners," this chapter serves as your comprehensive guide, offering a step-by-step roadmap to ensure a seamless initiation into the world of eBay reselling in 2024.

2.1 Setting Up Your eBay Seller Account in 2024:

The gateway to eBay success begins with the creation of your seller account. In 2024, eBay's onboarding process is not just a registration; it's an entry into a dynamic platform armed with cutting-edge tools. This section navigates the intricacies of setting up your eBay seller account, from the requisite documentation to the customization of your seller profile.

Understanding the latest updates in account setup ensures that newcomers are equipped with the most current information, setting the stage for a hassle-free initiation. Clear, step-by-step instructions accompanied by visual aids demystify the process, ensuring that your eBay seller account becomes a foundation for your reselling aspirations.

2.2 Navigating the Updated Interface and Features:

The landscape of eBay is not static; it evolves with the needs and preferences of its users. In 2024, sellers are greeted with an updated interface and a myriad of features designed to enhance the user experience. This section provides an in-depth exploration of the updated interface, ensuring that beginners navigate eBay's virtual corridors with confidence.

From understanding the revamped seller dashboard to harnessing the power of new tools, this segment sheds light on the features that form the backbone of your eBay selling experience. Navigating eBay's interface is not merely a technicality; it's a skill that empowers sellers to optimize their reselling strategies, making the most of the platform's offerings.

2.3 Building a Strong Foundation for Long-Term Success:

A successful eBay venture is not built on quicksand but on a solid foundation. This section goes beyond the initial setup, guiding beginners on how to cultivate a resilient and enduring reselling business. From crafting compelling product listings to implementing effective communication strategies, every aspect of building a strong foundation is covered.

This chapter encourages the adoption of best practices from the onset, emphasizing the significance of long-term vision over short-term gains. Whether you're a hobbyist looking to supplement your income or an aspiring entrepreneur aiming for full-time reselling, this blueprint equips beginners with the tools to build a robust foundation for sustained success.

As you delve into the nuances of getting started on eBay, consider this chapter not just a guide but a mentor, steering you through the pivotal initial steps of your reselling journey. The blueprint you forge today will become the cornerstone of your eBay success story tomorrow.

CHAPTER 3

Advanced eBay Strategies for Current Sellers

For those already navigating the dynamic landscape of eBay, success is not just about sustaining—it's about thriving. In "Advanced eBay Strategies for Current Sellers," this chapter unfolds as a playbook of innovative approaches tailored to the trends and technologies defining eBay in 2024.

3.1 Adapting Your Strategy to 2024 Trends:

Stagnation is the antithesis of success, and in the ever-evolving world of eCommerce, adaptation is the key. This section dives deep into the current trends shaping eBay in 2024, providing current sellers with a roadmap to not only stay relevant but to be at the forefront of industry shifts.

From the rising prominence of sustainable and ethical shopping to the integration of augmented reality in product visualization, understanding and embracing these trends is crucial for sellers aiming for sustained growth. Real-life examples and case studies illustrate how savvy sellers are capitalizing on trends, offering insights into replicable strategies that can elevate your eBay business.

3.2 Leveraging Cutting-Edge Technologies for Maximum Impact:

Technology is the backbone of eBay's evolution, and in 2024, sellers have a wealth of cutting-edge tools at their disposal. This section is a virtual toolbox, guiding current sellers on how to leverage the latest technologies for maximum impact on their reselling endeavors.

Explore the integration of artificial intelligence in inventory management, the potential of blockchain in enhancing transaction security, and the role of chatbots in providing stellar customer service. Understand how these technologies not only streamline operations but also contribute to a more personalized and efficient buyer experience. By mastering these tech-driven strategies, current sellers position themselves as pioneers in the eBay marketplace.

3.3 Optimizing Listings for Visibility and Sales:

In a crowded online marketplace, visibility is the gateway to sales. This segment is a masterclass in optimizing your eBay listings, ensuring that your products not only grab attention but convert browsers into buyers. Dive into the intricacies of crafting compelling product titles, creating engaging product descriptions, and utilizing high-quality visuals to captivate your audience.

Explore advanced SEO strategies to enhance the visibility of your listings within eBay's search algorithm. Uncover the art of strategic pricing, bundling, and cross-selling to maximize your revenue streams. Real-world examples showcase how sellers are implementing these optimization techniques with tangible success, providing inspiration for current sellers looking to enhance their listing game.

As you delve into "Advanced eBay Strategies for Current Sellers," consider this chapter as a portal to the future of your eBay success. It's not just about staying afloat; it's about riding the waves of innovation and technology to become a trailblazer in the ever-evolving world of eCommerce.

CHAPTER 4

Transforming Spare Time into Profit

In the pursuit of entrepreneurial success, time becomes a precious currency. "Transforming Spare Time into Profit" is not just a chapter; it's a strategic guide for eBay entrepreneurs navigating the delicate balance between building a home-based reselling business and managing other life commitments.

4.1 Balancing a Home-Based Reselling Business with Other Commitments:

For many eBay entrepreneurs, reselling is not their sole commitment. Juggling a home-based business with other responsibilities requires a delicate balancing act. This section explores practical strategies for maintaining equilibrium, whether you are a stay-at-home parent, a student, or someone with a full-time job.

Learn from the experiences of successful eBay sellers who have mastered the art of multitasking and discover strategies for integrating your reselling activities seamlessly into your daily routine. From setting realistic goals to leveraging productivity tools, this chapter provides insights to help you strike the right balance and transform your spare time into a profitable venture.

4.2 Time Management Strategies for eBay Entrepreneurs:

In the fast-paced world of eCommerce, effective time management is not just an asset; it's a competitive advantage. This segment delves into time management strategies tailored specifically for eBay entrepreneurs. Uncover techniques to prioritize tasks, set achievable deadlines, and leverage time-blocking to maximize productivity.

Explore the concept of batching similar tasks to streamline workflows and reduce cognitive load. Real-world examples illustrate how successful eBay entrepreneurs manage their time efficiently, offering actionable insights that can be applied to your own reselling journey. From the inception of your business to its scaling stages, effective time management remains a linchpin for success.

4.3 Tips for Maintaining Work-Life Balance:

In the quest for entrepreneurial success, maintaining work-life balance is often overlooked but is vital for sustained well-being. This section delves into actionable tips for eBay entrepreneurs to prevent burnout and foster a healthy equilibrium between work and personal life.

Discover mindfulness techniques to stay present, set boundaries to prevent overextension, and incorporate self-care practices into your routine. Insights from seasoned eBay sellers who have navigated the challenges of work-life balance provide valuable lessons for maintaining both personal and professional fulfillment.

As you immerse yourself in "Transforming Spare Time into Profit," envision not just a business thriving in the margins of your schedule but a harmonious integration of reselling into your lifestyle. This chapter is more than a guide; it's a companion for eBay entrepreneurs seeking not only financial success but also a balanced and fulfilling life.

CHAPTER 5

The Reselling Revolution: Proven Techniques for Profitability

Welcome to the heart of the reselling revolution, where the secrets of top eBay sellers are unveiled, strategies for sourcing profitable products are dissected, and the art of building and managing your inventory effectively is mastered. This chapter is not just a guide; it's a manifesto for profitability in the reselling realm.

5.1 Unveiling Secrets of Top eBay Sellers:

Behind every successful eBay seller lies a set of strategies and secrets that contribute to their triumph. This section peels back the curtain, revealing the proven techniques employed by top eBay sellers. From mastering customer service to leveraging marketing channels effectively, learn how these sellers have navigated challenges and emerged as industry leaders.

Case studies showcase real-world applications of these secrets, providing invaluable insights for resellers looking to elevate their game. Uncover the nuances of effective communication, customer retention, and brand building, and let the success stories of top eBay sellers inspire your journey in the reselling revolution.

5.2 Strategies for Sourcing Profitable Products:

In the reselling landscape, success begins with the products you choose to sell. This segment delves into strategies for sourcing profitable products, guiding resellers on how to identify lucrative niches and capitalize on market trends. Explore the art of product research, from leveraging eBay's data analytics tools to scouring external platforms for hidden gems.

Discover how successful resellers navigate the complexities of product sourcing, from understanding consumer demand to evaluating competition. Whether you're a novice seeking your first profitable product or an experienced seller expanding your product line, these strategies are your compass in the reselling revolution.

5.3 Building and Managing Your Inventory Effectively:

An effective inventory is the backbone of a successful reselling business. This section unravels the intricacies of building and managing your inventory with precision. Learn how to optimize stock levels, implement efficient storage solutions, and strategically diversify your product offerings.

Case studies highlight the inventory management practices of successful eBay sellers, offering practical tips for avoiding overstock or stockouts. Explore the importance of tracking product performance, adjusting inventory based on market trends, and fostering a dynamic inventory strategy that adapts to the evolving landscape of the reselling revolution.

As you immerse yourself in "The Reselling Revolution," envision not just a business but a dynamic and profitable enterprise. This chapter is your manual for navigating the reselling realm with expertise, mastering the proven techniques employed by industry leaders, and carving your path to profitability in the exciting world of eBay reselling.

CHAPTER 6

eBay 2.0: Maximizing Profits with Tech-Savvy Approaches

Welcome to the era of eBay 2.0, where resellers transcend traditional boundaries and embrace cutting-edge tools and technologies to maximize profits. This chapter is your gateway to exploring the latest innovations on eBay, integrating artificial intelligence and automation for unparalleled efficiency, and gaining tech-driven competitive advantages to stay ahead in the reselling game.

6.1 Exploring the Latest eBay Tools and Technologies:

eBay, in its continuous evolution, introduces a plethora of tools and technologies aimed at enhancing the reselling experience. This section is your backstage pass to explore these latest features, from revamped seller dashboards to advanced analytics tools. Understand how to leverage these tools to gain insights into market trends, track customer behavior, and optimize your reselling strategy.

Real-life examples showcase how top resellers integrate these tools into their daily operations, providing a blueprint for maximizing efficiency. Whether you're a seasoned seller or a newcomer, this chapter equips you with the knowledge to navigate eBay's technological landscape and unlock the full potential of its latest offerings.

6.2 Integrating AI and Automation for Efficient Operations:

In the age of eBay 2.0, artificial intelligence and automation emerge as game-changers for resellers. This segment delves into the strategic integration of AI and automation to streamline operations, enhance customer experiences, and elevate overall efficiency. Explore how AI-powered chatbots can revolutionize customer service, automating responses and providing instant support.

Learn how automation tools can simplify tasks like order processing, inventory management, and pricing adjustments. Case studies illustrate how resellers effectively implement these technologies, showcasing tangible improvements in time management and operational effectiveness. As eBay evolves, staying ahead requires a mastery of AI and automation, and this chapter serves as your guide to incorporating these tech-savvy approaches into your reselling toolkit.

6.3 Staying Ahead with Tech-Driven Competitive Advantages:

In the fast-paced world of eCommerce, staying ahead requires more than just keeping up – it demands proactive adoption of tech-driven competitive advantages. This section unveils strategies employed by top resellers to gain an edge, from using data analytics to optimize pricing strategies to utilizing targeted advertising campaigns powered by AI.

Explore the role of personalized recommendations, dynamic pricing algorithms, and predictive analytics in outsmarting the competition. Understand how resellers leverage technology not just for operational efficiency but to enhance the overall customer journey. By staying abreast of the latest technological trends, you position yourself not just as a participant in the eBay 2.0 revolution but as a trailblazer, leading the way in the reselling landscape.

As you delve into "eBay 2.0: Maximizing Profits with Tech-Savvy Approaches," envision not just a reselling business but a tech-driven enterprise poised for success in the future of eCommerce. This chapter is your compass for navigating the intersection of technology and reselling, ensuring that you not only adapt but thrive in the dynamic landscape of eBay 2.0.

CHAPTER 7

Mastering the eBay Ecosystem

In the intricate world of eBay, mastery extends beyond the act of selling. This chapter unveils the holistic view of eBay's ecosystem, guiding resellers to transcend the conventional boundaries and explore additional features that amplify exposure. Discover strategies for cross-promotion and collaborations that not only elevate your products but position you as a master of the complete eBay landscape.

7.1 Beyond Selling: Understanding eBay's Entire Ecosystem:

eBay is more than just a marketplace; it's a dynamic ecosystem encompassing a myriad of features designed to empower resellers. This section broadens your perspective, encouraging you to explore eBay's entire ecosystem. From understanding the nuances of eBay Stores to harnessing the power of promoted listings, gain insights into how these additional features can amplify your brand visibility and attract a broader audience.

Real-world examples showcase how resellers have harnessed the potential of eBay's ecosystem to create a cohesive and immersive brand experience. This chapter is not merely about selling products; it's about positioning yourself within the expansive eBay ecosystem for sustained success and recognition.

7.2 Utilizing Additional Features for Increased Exposure:

In eBay's diverse ecosystem, additional features become tools for resellers to enhance their visibility and reach. This segment unveils these features and provides a strategic guide on how to utilize them effectively. Explore the benefits of eBay Plus, delve into the intricacies of eBay's Global Shipping Program, and understand the impact of offering free shipping on your listings.

Case studies illustrate how resellers strategically leverage these features to attract more buyers, build trust, and create a positive shopping experience. By mastering these additional features, you not only optimize your selling strategy but become a savvy navigator of the eBay landscape.

7.3 Strategies for Cross-Promotion and Collaborations:

Collaboration is a cornerstone of success in the reselling realm. This section explores the art of cross-promotion and collaborations, showcasing how resellers can join forces to amplify their reach and tap into new markets. Understand the power of strategic partnerships, whether it's collaborating with other eBay sellers or cross-promoting with influencers and complementary brands.

Real-life examples demonstrate how these collaborations result in mutually beneficial outcomes, from increased exposure to expanded customer bases. This chapter invites you to think beyond the confines of individual listings and explore the synergies that arise from collaboration, positioning you as a master of strategic partnerships within the eBay ecosystem.

As you delve into "Mastering the eBay Ecosystem," envision not just a seller navigating the marketplace but a master of the entire eBay landscape. This chapter empowers you to go beyond the basics, explore the richness of eBay's features, and strategically position yourself for sustained success within the dynamic eBay ecosystem.

CHAPTER 8

Overcoming Challenges in 2024

In the ever-evolving landscape of eBay reselling, challenges are inevitable, but mastery lies in the ability to overcome them. This chapter addresses the common pain points experienced by eBay sellers in 2024, provides guidance on navigating policy changes and updates, and equips resellers with effective troubleshooting and problem-solving strategies.

8.1 Addressing Common Pain Points of eBay Sellers:

Success is often accompanied by challenges, and eBay sellers are no strangers to hurdles that may impede their journey. This section empathetically addresses the common pain points experienced by eBay sellers in 2024, from dealing with shipping complexities to managing customer disputes and handling returns.

Through practical insights and real-world examples, this chapter serves as a guide for resellers to navigate these challenges effectively. Learn strategies for proactive problem-solving, effective communication, and fostering positive customer relationships, transforming pain points into opportunities for growth and improvement.

8.2 Navigating Policy Changes and Updates:

In the dynamic world of eCommerce, policies and guidelines can undergo frequent changes, presenting a challenge for sellers to stay compliant. This segment provides a comprehensive approach to navigating policy changes and updates on eBay in 2024. From understanding new selling standards to adapting to updated fee structures, resellers are guided on how to stay informed and compliant.

Case studies highlight how successful eBay sellers not only adapt to policy changes but leverage them to their advantage. Whether you're a seasoned seller or a newcomer, this chapter ensures you are equipped with the knowledge and strategies to navigate the evolving policy landscape on eBay.

8.3 Troubleshooting and Problem-Solving Strategies:

Every eBay seller encounters unexpected challenges that require swift and effective resolution. This section unveils troubleshooting and problem-solving strategies to equip resellers with the skills to address issues as they arise. Explore techniques for identifying the root cause of problems, implementing quick fixes, and preventing similar issues in the future.

Real-world scenarios provide valuable insights into the problem-solving approaches employed by successful eBay sellers. By adopting a proactive mindset and embracing challenges as opportunities to enhance your reselling strategy, you position yourself as a resilient and adaptive entrepreneur in the dynamic eBay landscape.

As you delve into "Overcoming Challenges in 2024," envision not just a guide to addressing issues but a manual for transforming challenges into stepping stones for success. This chapter empowers eBay sellers to navigate the complexities of the reselling landscape with resilience, confidence, and a strategic problem-solving mindset.

CHAPTER 9

Turning Ambition into Action: A Roadmap for Side Hustlers

For side hustlers venturing into the world of eBay reselling, ambition is the spark, but action is the flame. In this pivotal chapter, discover a comprehensive roadmap for transforming ambition into tangible success. Learn how to implement the blueprint for success, set realistic goals and milestones, and gradually scale your eBay business to achieve the side hustle of your dreams.

9.1 Implementing the Blueprint for Success:

Your journey from ambition to action begins with a clear blueprint for success. This section guides side hustlers on the implementation of the strategies outlined throughout the book. Whether you're a newcomer or a seasoned seller, understand how to tailor the insights and techniques to your unique situation, creating a personalized roadmap for success.

Real-life examples showcase how other side hustlers have successfully implemented the blueprint, offering inspiration and practical tips for navigating the initial stages of your reselling venture. By translating theory into action, you set the stage for a side hustle that not only aligns with your ambitions but flourishes in the dynamic eBay marketplace.

9.2 Setting Realistic Goals and Milestones:

Ambition thrives on clear goals and achievable milestones. This segment delves into the art of goal-setting for side hustlers, emphasizing the importance of realism and adaptability. Learn how to define short-term and long-term goals that align with your aspirations and the unique demands of your side hustle.

Through practical exercises and guidance, this chapter assists side hustlers in establishing milestones that act as stepping stones toward overarching success. By setting realistic expectations and celebrating incremental victories, you create a sustainable and motivating framework for your eBay reselling journey.

9.3 Scaling Your eBay Business Gradually:

Scaling a side hustle is a delicate balance between ambition and practicality. This section provides a roadmap for side hustlers to gradually expand their eBay businesses. Explore strategies for diversifying product offerings, expanding target markets, and increasing operational efficiency without overwhelming your capacity.

Case studies highlight successful side hustlers who have effectively scaled their eBay businesses, offering insights into the challenges they faced and the strategies they employed. By embracing a gradual scaling approach, side hustlers ensure the sustainability and long-term success of their reselling endeavors.

As you embark on the final leg of your eBay reselling journey, envision not just the realization of your ambitions but the strategic implementation of a roadmap for sustainable success. This chapter is your companion, offering guidance and inspiration as you turn ambition into action and transform your eBay side hustle into a thriving and fulfilling venture.

CHAPTER 10

Branding and Marketing Your eBay Business

In the dynamic realm of eBay reselling, crafting a compelling brand identity and implementing effective marketing strategies are paramount. Chapter 10 unveils the secrets of successful eBay sellers who have mastered the art of branding and marketing. Explore how to craft a unique brand identity, implement strategies to boost visibility, leverage social media for brand promotion, and gain insights from case studies showcasing eBay sellers with strong branding.

10.1 Crafting a Unique Brand Identity for Your eBay Store:

Your eBay store is not just a collection of products; it's a brand with a distinct identity. This section guides resellers through the process of crafting a unique brand identity that resonates with their target audience. Understand the elements of brand identity, from designing a memorable logo to creating a cohesive visual style.

Through practical exercises and real-world examples, learn how successful eBay sellers have differentiated themselves in a crowded marketplace by establishing a strong brand identity. By infusing personality and authenticity into your brand, you create a lasting impression that goes beyond individual transactions.

10.2 Implementing Effective Marketing Strategies to Boost Visibility:

Visibility is the lifeblood of successful reselling. This segment dives into effective marketing strategies tailored for eBay sellers. Explore techniques for optimizing product listings, utilizing eBay promotions, and harnessing the power of email marketing to boost visibility and attract a broader audience.

Case studies highlight resellers who have implemented these strategies with tangible success, providing inspiration and practical tips for boosting visibility in the competitive eBay landscape. By mastering these marketing strategies, you position your eBay business for increased exposure and potential growth.

10.3 Leveraging Social Media and Online Platforms for Brand Promotion:

In the digital age, social media and online platforms are powerful tools for brand promotion. This section explores how eBay sellers can leverage social media to enhance brand visibility, engage with their audience, and drive traffic to their eBay stores. Understand the nuances of content creation, community building, and strategic social media advertising.

Real-world examples showcase how successful eBay sellers use platforms like Instagram, Facebook, and Pinterest to amplify their brand presence. By building a cross-channel online presence, you not only reach a wider audience but also foster a community around your brand.

10.4 Case Studies: Successful eBay Sellers with Strong Branding:

What better way to understand the impact of branding and marketing than through real-life success stories? This chapter concludes with in-depth case studies of eBay sellers who have successfully established strong branding. Explore their journeys, the challenges they overcame, and the strategies they employed to build a memorable and recognizable brand on eBay.

By delving into these case studies, resellers gain practical insights and inspiration, discovering how branding is not just a theoretical concept but a tangible and transformative aspect of eBay success.

As you immerse yourself in the final chapter of this reselling journey, envision not just a store but a brand that resonates, captivates, and thrives in the dynamic eBay ecosystem. This chapter is your guide to mastering the art of branding and marketing, ensuring that your eBay business not only survives but flourishes in the ever-evolving landscape of online retail.

CHAPTER 11

Customer Service Excellence in 2024

In the intricate tapestry of eBay success, customer service is the golden thread that weaves together satisfaction, loyalty, and repeat business. Chapter 11 delves into the pivotal role of customer service in the reselling journey, guiding eBay sellers on implementing proactive communication strategies, resolving issues adeptly, handling customer feedback constructively, and building long-term relationships for sustained success.

11.1 The Role of Customer Service in eBay Success:

Customer service is not merely a component of eBay success; it is the cornerstone upon which lasting success is built. This section illuminates the critical role customer service plays in the reselling ecosystem. Understand how exceptional customer service goes beyond transactional interactions, creating a positive customer experience that transcends individual purchases.

Explore the impact of customer service on buyer satisfaction, positive feedback, and word-of-mouth recommendations. Through real-world examples, grasp the significance of customer service excellence in fostering trust, loyalty, and the foundation for repeat business.

11.2 Implementing Proactive Communication Strategies:

Proactive communication is the bedrock of stellar customer service. This segment provides insights into strategies for initiating communication with buyers, setting clear expectations, and providing timely updates throughout the purchase journey. Learn how to leverage automated messages, personalized communication, and transparent policies to enhance the overall buyer experience.

Case studies highlight the impact of proactive communication on customer satisfaction and how it contributes to a positive seller reputation. By mastering proactive communication, eBay sellers not only address buyer inquiries but also create an environment where customers feel valued and supported.

11.3 Resolving Issues and Handling Customer Feedback:

In the world of reselling, issues and feedback are inevitable, but how they are handled defines the trajectory of success. This section equips eBay sellers with effective strategies for resolving issues promptly, addressing customer concerns, and transforming negative feedback into opportunities for improvement.

Real-world examples showcase how successful eBay sellers turn challenging situations into positive experiences through proactive issue resolution. By adopting a customer-centric approach, sellers not only salvage relationships but also enhance their reputation as reliable and responsive sellers.

11.4 Building Long-Term Customer Relationships for Repeat Business:

Beyond individual transactions, the ability to build long-term customer relationships is a hallmark of reselling excellence. This segment explores strategies for creating a customer-centric culture that encourages repeat business. Learn the art of personalized service, loyalty programs, and ongoing engagement to turn one-time buyers into loyal customers.

Case studies of eBay sellers who have successfully built long-term customer relationships provide inspiration and actionable insights. By prioritizing customer relationships, sellers not only secure repeat business but also foster a community of advocates who amplify the brand through positive word-of-mouth.

As you navigate the final chapter of this reselling guide, envision not just transactions but relationships that endure and flourish. This chapter is your guide to mastering customer service excellence in 2024, ensuring that every interaction on eBay becomes a stepping stone towards sustained success and a legacy of satisfied customers.

CHAPTER 12

Financial Management for eBay Entrepreneurs

In the intricate dance of eBay entrepreneurship, financial management takes center stage. Chapter 12 serves as a comprehensive guide for eBay sellers, providing insights on creating a budget, meticulous tracking of expenses and profits, understanding tax considerations in 2024, and implementing strategies for financial growth and sustainability.

12.1 Creating a Budget for Your eBay Business:

The foundation of financial success is a well-crafted budget. This section delves into the nuances of creating a budget tailored to the unique needs of an eBay business. Explore how to allocate funds for inventory, marketing, and operational expenses while ensuring a healthy margin for profits.

Through practical exercises and real-world examples, learn how successful eBay entrepreneurs use budgets not just as financial guides but as strategic tools for decision-making. By crafting a comprehensive budget, sellers gain control over their financial landscape and set the stage for sustainable growth.

12.2 Tracking Expenses, Profits, and Cash Flow:

In the dynamic world of reselling, meticulous tracking of finances is not just a best practice; it's a necessity. This segment provides a roadmap for eBay entrepreneurs to track expenses, monitor profits, and manage cash flow effectively. Understand the importance of accurate record-keeping, utilizing accounting tools, and establishing financial benchmarks.

Real-life examples illustrate how detailed financial tracking empowers sellers to make informed decisions, identify areas for improvement, and maintain a healthy financial position. By mastering the art of financial tracking, eBay entrepreneurs ensure that every transaction contributes to the overall health of their business.

12.3 Tax Considerations for eBay Sellers in 2024:

Navigating the labyrinth of tax considerations is a crucial aspect of financial management. This section provides insights into the specific tax considerations eBay sellers need to be aware of in 2024. From understanding tax deductions and credits to staying compliant with evolving tax regulations, sellers gain a comprehensive understanding of their tax obligations.

Case studies showcase how successful eBay entrepreneurs approach tax planning, ensuring that financial decisions align with both business growth and compliance with tax laws. By staying informed and proactive, sellers can optimize their financial strategy in a way that minimizes tax liability while maximizing profitability.

12.4 Strategies for Financial Growth and Sustainability:

Financial management is not just about maintaining the status quo; it's about fostering growth and sustainability. This segment explores strategies for financial growth, from reinvesting profits strategically to diversifying revenue streams. Learn how to leverage financial insights to identify opportunities for expansion and navigate challenges effectively.

Real-world examples highlight how successful eBay entrepreneurs have implemented these strategies to achieve sustainable financial growth. By adopting a forward-looking approach to financial management, sellers position themselves not just for success in the present but for long-term resilience in the dynamic landscape of eBay entrepreneurship.

As you embark on the final chapter of this reselling journey, envision not just transactions but a thriving and financially resilient eBay business. This chapter is your compass for mastering financial management, ensuring that every financial decision contributes to the growth and sustainability of your eBay entrepreneurship venture in 2024 and beyond.

CHAPTER 13

Navigating International Markets on eBay

In the interconnected world of eBay, expanding beyond borders is not just an opportunity; it's a strategic imperative. Chapter 13 is your guide to navigating international markets on eBay, unlocking the benefits of global selling, overcoming challenges in the realm of global eCommerce, understanding the intricacies of international shipping and customs, and tailoring your listings to resonate with a diverse and global audience.

13.1 Expanding Your Reach: Benefits of Selling Internationally:

The decision to sell internationally is not just a geographical expansion; it's an elevation of your eBay business to new heights. This section explores the myriad benefits of selling internationally, from tapping into larger customer bases to diversifying revenue streams and fostering brand recognition on a global scale.

Real-world examples showcase how eBay sellers have harnessed the power of international markets to amplify their success. By expanding your reach beyond borders, you not only access new opportunities but position your brand as a global player in the ever-evolving eCommerce landscape.

13.2 Overcoming Challenges in Global eCommerce:

Entering the global eCommerce arena is not without its challenges. This segment equips eBay sellers with strategies for overcoming common obstacles in global markets, from language barriers to varying consumer behaviors and regulatory complexities.

Case studies provide insights into how successful eBay sellers have navigated and triumphed over challenges, offering a blueprint for newcomers venturing into the global eCommerce space. By understanding and proactively addressing these challenges, sellers can ensure a smooth transition into the world of international markets.

13.3 Understanding International Shipping and Customs:

The logistics of international selling require a nuanced understanding of shipping and customs procedures. This section unravels the intricacies of international shipping, exploring cost-effective shipping options, fulfillment strategies, and navigating the complexities of customs regulations.

Through practical guidance and real-life examples, sellers gain insights into how to optimize their shipping processes for international markets. By demystifying international shipping and customs, eBay sellers ensure a seamless and reliable experience for customers around the world.

13.4 Tailoring Your Listings for a Global Audience:

Selling internationally is not just about reaching new customers; it's about speaking their language, both literally and figuratively. This segment delves into the art of tailoring your listings for a global audience, from crafting compelling product descriptions that transcend language barriers to incorporating cultural nuances in your marketing approach.

Explore strategies for localization, effective use of international keywords, and adapting visuals to resonate with diverse cultural preferences. Real-world examples highlight how successful eBay sellers have customized their listings to create a global appeal. By tailoring your approach, you not only attract international customers but also foster a sense of connection and trust across borders.

As you venture into the expansive world of international markets on eBay, envision not just transactions but a global community of customers who value your products and brand. This chapter is your passport to success in international selling, providing insights and strategies to navigate the complexities and embrace the opportunities that come with expanding your eBay business beyond domestic borders.

CHAPTER 14

Staying Ethical and Sustainable in Your eBay Business

In the evolving landscape of eBay entrepreneurship, ethical and sustainable practices are not just commendable; they are integral to long-term success. Chapter 14 guides eBay sellers on the importance of ethical business practices, the implementation of sustainability in their reselling endeavors, the creation of a responsible supply chain, and strategies for appealing to eco-conscious consumers on eBay.

14.1 The Importance of Ethical Business Practices:

Ethical business practices are the moral compass that guides your eBay journey. This section explores the significance of conducting business with integrity, transparency, and fairness. Understand how ethical practices contribute to a positive brand image, customer trust, and long-term success in the reselling landscape.

Real-world examples showcase how eBay sellers have built thriving businesses by prioritizing ethics in their operations. By embracing ethical standards, sellers not only contribute to a more responsible business environment but also position themselves as trustworthy partners in the eyes of customers.

14.2 Implementing Sustainability in Your Reselling Business:

Sustainability is no longer a trend; it's a fundamental responsibility of businesses in the 21st century. This segment delves into the practical aspects of implementing sustainability in your reselling business. From eco-friendly packaging to responsible sourcing of materials, discover strategies for reducing your environmental footprint and fostering a sustainable business model.

Case studies highlight how eBay sellers have successfully integrated sustainability into their operations, gaining not only positive recognition but also contributing to environmental conservation. By adopting sustainable practices, sellers align their businesses with the growing global consciousness towards eco-friendly and socially responsible consumerism.

14.3 Building a Responsible Supply Chain:

The supply chain is the lifeline of any reselling business, and making it responsible is a key step toward ethical entrepreneurship. This section provides insights into building a responsible supply chain, from choosing ethical suppliers to ensuring fair labor practices. Understand how a transparent and responsible supply chain enhances the credibility of your business and appeals to conscientious consumers.

Practical guidance and examples showcase how successful eBay sellers have navigated the complexities of supply chain responsibility, creating a positive impact on both their brand and the wider community. By building a responsible supply chain, sellers contribute to a fair and sustainable ecosystem.

14.4 Appealing to Eco-Conscious Consumers on eBay:

Eco-conscious consumers are a growing demographic with a keen interest in supporting businesses that share their values. This segment explores strategies for appealing to this audience on eBay. From incorporating eco-friendly messaging in your listings to showcasing your commitment to sustainability, discover how to attract and retain eco-conscious customers.

Real-life examples illustrate how eBay sellers have successfully tapped into the eco-conscious market, creating a loyal customer base that values their ethical and sustainable practices. By aligning your brand with the values of eco-conscious consumers, sellers not only drive sales but also contribute to positive change in consumer behavior.

As you embark on the ethical and sustainable journey in your eBay business, envision not just transactions but a positive impact on the planet and society. This chapter is your guide to staying ethical and sustainable in the reselling landscape, providing actionable insights and strategies to foster a business that not only thrives economically but also contributes to a better and more responsible world.

CONCLUSION

eBay Success in 2024

As we conclude this comprehensive journey through the dynamic landscape of eBay entrepreneurship in 2024, let's take a moment to recap the key takeaways that will shape your path to success. From understanding the power of eBay in the modern eCommerce ecosystem to mastering advanced strategies, building a resilient brand, and navigating global markets, each chapter has been a compass guiding you through the intricacies of reselling on eBay.

Recap of Key Takeaways:

eBay Advantage in 2024: Delve into the power of eBay in the modern eCommerce landscape, capitalizing on opportunities and overcoming challenges.

- **Getting Started Blueprint**: Lay a strong foundation by setting up your eBay seller account, navigating the interface, and ensuring long-term success.

- **Advanced Strategies**: Adapt your approach to 2024 trends, leverage technology, and optimize listings for maximum visibility and sales.

- **Transforming Spare Time into Profit**: Balance your home-based reselling business with effective time management strategies, ensuring a harmonious work-life equilibrium.

- **Reselling Revolution**: Unveil the secrets of top eBay sellers, master strategies for sourcing profitable products, and effectively manage your inventory.

- **eBay 2.0**: Maximize profits with tech-savvy approaches, exploring the latest eBay tools, integrating AI, and staying ahead in a tech-driven landscape.

- **Mastering the eBay Ecosystem**: Go beyond selling and understand eBay's entire ecosystem, utilizing additional features for increased exposure and exploring cross-promotion strategies.

- **Overcoming Challenges in 2024**: Address common pain points, navigate policy changes, and implement effective troubleshooting and problem-solving strategies.

- **Turning Ambition into Action**: Implement the blueprint for success, set realistic goals, and gradually scale your eBay business for sustained growth.

- **Branding and Marketing**: Craft a unique brand identity, implement effective marketing strategies, leverage social media, and learn from successful sellers with strong branding.

- **Customer Service Excellence**: Recognize the pivotal role of customer service, implement proactive communication, resolve issues adeptly, and build long-term customer relationships.

- **Financial Management**: Create a budget, track expenses, understand tax considerations, and implement strategies for financial growth and sustainability.

- **Navigating International Markets**: Expand your reach globally, overcome challenges in global eCommerce, understand international shipping and customs, and tailor your listings for a global audience.

- **Staying Ethical and Sustainable**: Embrace ethical business practices, implement sustainability, build a responsible supply chain, and appeal to eco-conscious consumers.

Encouragement and Inspiration for eBay Success in 2024:

Embarking on the eBay journey demands dedication, resilience, and a commitment to continuous improvement. As you navigate the ever-changing eCommerce landscape, remember that success is not just about transactions but about creating a lasting impact. Your ambition is the fuel that propels you forward, and every challenge is an opportunity for growth.

In the fast-paced world of reselling, staying informed, adapting to trends, and embracing innovation are your greatest allies. Draw inspiration from your own progress, celebrate your achievements, and view challenges not as obstacles but as stepping stones toward eBay success in 2024 and beyond.

Invitation to Join a Community of eBay Entrepreneurs:

Your journey as an eBay entrepreneur is not solitary. As you reflect on the knowledge gained from this guide, consider joining a community of like-minded individuals who share your passion for reselling on eBay. Connect with fellow entrepreneurs, exchange insights, and tap into the collective wisdom of a community that understands the unique challenges and triumphs of eBay entrepreneurship.

Whether through online forums, social media groups, or local meetups, the camaraderie of a community can be a powerful catalyst for growth. Share your experiences, seek advice, and contribute to the collective knowledge that propels eBay entrepreneurs to new heights.

As the concluding chapter of this guide, the invitation is clear: embrace your role as part of a thriving community of eBay entrepreneurs. Together, we navigate the ever-changing seas of eCommerce, drawing strength and inspiration from each other as we collectively shape the future of eBay entrepreneurship in 2024 and beyond.

Here's to your continued success on eBay!

APPENDIX

Your Comprehensive Toolkit for eBay Success

Congratulations on completing this insightful journey through the world of eBay entrepreneurship! As you embark on your own reselling adventure, the Appendix serves as your go-to toolkit, providing additional resources, tools, reading suggestions, and quick reference guides to enhance your eBay success.

1. Additional Resources and Tools:

Here, you'll find a curated list of additional resources and tools to further empower your eBay journey. Whether you're seeking advanced analytics tools, inventory management solutions, or expert insights, these resources will complement the knowledge gained from this guide.

- ➤ eBay Seller Center: Your hub for official eBay resources, guides, and updates.
- ➤ Terapeak: Leverage advanced analytics for eBay market research.
- ➤ Inventory Management Tools: Explore tools like Sellbrite, Skubana, or ChannelAdvisor for efficient inventory management.
- ➤ eBay Community: Engage with fellow sellers, ask questions, and share experiences in the eBay Community forums.

2. Glossary of eBay Terms:

Unlock the language of eBay with this comprehensive glossary. Whether you're a newcomer or a seasoned seller, understanding these terms will enhance your communication and comprehension within the eBay ecosystem.

- ➤ Bid Sniping: The practice of placing a bid at the last possible moment to prevent others from outbidding you.
- ➤ BIN (Buy It Now): A fixed-price listing that allows buyers to purchase items immediately.

- ➢ Feedback Score: A numerical score based on buyer and seller feedback, indicating reputation.
- ➢ Listing Optimization: Strategies to improve the visibility and performance of your product listings.

3. Quick Reference Guides for Common eBay Procedures:

Navigate eBay procedures with ease using these quick reference guides. From setting up your seller account to managing returns, these guides provide step-by-step instructions for common eBay tasks.

- ➢ Setting Up Your eBay Seller Account: A step-by-step guide for creating and optimizing your seller account.
- ➢ Optimizing Product Listings: Learn the essentials of creating compelling and effective product listings.
- ➢ Handling Returns on eBay: A guide to navigating the returns process and maintaining positive customer relations.
- ➢ Utilizing Promotions: Strategies for running effective promotions to boost sales.

4. Reading Suggestions for Continued Learning:

Feed your entrepreneurial spirit with additional reading suggestions. These books cover a range of topics, from eCommerce strategies to business mindset, offering valuable insights to further fuel your eBay success.

- ❖ "The Lean Startup" by Eric Ries: Learn how to build a successful startup by applying lean and agile principles.
- ❖ "Crushing It!" by Gary Vaynerchuk: Gain insights into personal branding and leveraging social media for business success.
- ❖ "The 4-Hour Workweek" by Timothy Ferriss: Explore strategies for achieving more with less, optimizing your business and lifestyle.

Closing Note:

As you utilize the tools, explore the resources, and continue your journey in the world of eBay entrepreneurship, remember that growth is a continuous process. Stay curious, embrace challenges as opportunities, and leverage the knowledge gained from this guide alongside the additional resources provided in the Appendix.

May your eBay venture be filled with prosperity, learning, and a thriving community of fellow entrepreneurs. Happy reselling!